Long-Form Video Production for YouTube

Create High-Retention Videos Using Scripts, Structure & Studio-Quality Techniques

By Joe Correa

Published by Live Stronger Faster

This book is for educational and informational purposes only. The author and publisher are not engaged in rendering legal, financial, or other professional advice. Readers should consult a qualified professional before making any financial decisions.

First Edition

Table of Contents

Introduction

Long-form content is the heart of YouTube—the place where depth, storytelling, education, and real transformation happen. While short-form videos are fast, fun, and essential for reaching new audiences, long-form videos are where trust is built, expertise is proven, and businesses are grown. People may discover you on Instagram Reels or TikTok, but it is your long-form YouTube videos that convince them to stay, subscribe, binge, buy, and become lifelong fans. This book is designed to turn you into a master of long-form video production even if you're filming from home, working with minimal equipment, or feel like you're still learning the basics. You're about to discover the systems, scripts, structures, and creative techniques used by top YouTubers to hold attention for 5, 10, 15, or even 45 minutes—consistently, repeatably, and profitably.

Creating long-form content that works in today's algorithm is not about talking for a long time. It is about *earning* every second of watch time through structure, pacing, clarity, and viewer psychology. YouTube is the only platform where time spent watching is more valuable than views alone, and the creators who understand this are the ones who grow the fastest. High retention leads to exponential recommendations, rapid subscriber growth, and monetization opportunities that short-form platforms simply cannot match. YouTube rewards creators who keep people watching, and this book will show you exactly how to create videos that are not just watchable, but addictive—videos that feel like they "flow," videos viewers finish without even realizing they've watched 20 minutes, videos that make people say in the comments: *"I don't know how I got here, but I'm staying."*

At the core of great long-form video is a strong structure. Most creators struggle because they press record without a blueprint. They ramble, repeat themselves, get stuck, or lose energy halfway through. Viewers can feel this immediately. Long-form videos require the same level of planning as a mini-documentary, podcast, or short lesson. The good news is that once you master structure, everything becomes easier: filming becomes faster, editing becomes cleaner, your message becomes clearer, and your videos finally start performing the way they should. In this book, you'll learn how to build YouTube-ready structures for tutorials, commentary videos, interviews, reviews, vlogs, educational content, documentary-style videos, and hybrid formats that blend storytelling with information. Once you understand these frameworks, you will be able to create powerful long-form content on command—without struggling, overthinking, or feeling stuck.

But long-form success is not just about what you say—it's about how you say it, how it looks, and most importantly, how it *sounds*. Audio quality matters more in long-form than short-form because viewers spend much more time listening than watching. A viewer will forgive imperfect lighting, but they will never forgive bad audio. This book will teach you how to achieve studio-quality sound on any budget, whether you're using a USB microphone, a wireless lav, a shotgun mic, or even just your smartphone with the right setup. You'll also learn how to create visual depth, use natural light to your advantage, set up home studios that look professional without costing much, and incorporate b-roll, text overlays, graphics, and transitions that make your videos feel dynamic and polished—even if you edit everything yourself.

Long-form videos succeed when they combine *intention* with *immersion*. Your viewer must feel guided, entertained, informed, and emotionally connected throughout the entire experience. This is where pacing becomes essential. Many creators speak too slowly, rely on filler words, or jump too quickly between ideas without transitions. Others flood their videos with unnecessary information or long pauses that reduce watch time. In this book, you'll learn the principles of viewer pacing used by top YouTubers—the perfect balance between speed and clarity, when to pause, when to add b-roll, how to use camera movement, how to vary shot angles, and how to keep your audience fully engaged from start to finish. Long-form pacing is a skill, and once you learn it, your videos immediately feel more professional and easier to watch.

Another major component of long-form success is scripting. Unlike short-form videos, where loose outlines can work, long-form videos collapse without structure. You don't need to memorize every line—you just need a proven system that keeps the content organized and the message impactful. In this book, you will learn how to write scripts using AI, how to build outlines that allow for natural delivery, how to structure educational content so viewers stay engaged, how to add stories that improve retention, and how to use emotional sequencing to create powerful viewer experiences. You'll also learn how to craft intros that stop viewers from clicking away, mid-video re-hooks that pull attention back, and endings that drive subscribers, comments, and watch-time-boosting binge sessions.

Finally, this book will prepare you for the long-term game that makes YouTube such a powerful platform. Every long-form video you publish becomes a digital asset that can earn income for years. Your goal is not to upload randomly but to create a content library—structured, strategic, evergreen, searchable, and optimized for both humans and the algorithm. Long-form content is the foundation of sustainable growth because it builds trust at scale, positions you as an authority, and creates more opportunities for monetization than any other form of content. As you move through this book, you will learn how to plan long-form videos that support your brand, your business, and your future as a creator.

By the time you finish this introduction, you will understand why long-form video is the most powerful, profitable, and enduring form of content online. You'll be ready to create videos that rise above the noise, videos viewers actually finish, videos YouTube loves to recommend, and videos that grow your audience and income for years to come. Whether you're teaching, inspiring, reviewing, documenting, storytelling, analyzing, entertaining, or building a community, this book will give you everything you need to film high-retention, studio-quality long-form videos—no expensive equipment, big team, or Hollywood training required. You're about to unlock the true potential of YouTube. Let's begin.

Chapter 1

The Foundations of High-Retention YouTube Videos

Long-form videos succeed or fail based on one thing above all else: retention. The longer you can keep someone watching, the faster your channel grows, the more the algorithm pushes your content, and the greater the trust you build with your audience. But retention isn't an accident. It is engineered—strategically, deliberately, and predictably—through structure, pacing, clarity, and viewer psychology. Chapter 1 lays the foundation you will use for every long-form video you ever create. Whether you're filming tutorials, storytelling, reviews, commentary, vlogs, interviews, or educational content, the principles in this chapter apply universally and will support the success of every future technique you learn in this book.

At a fundamental level, high-retention videos respect the viewer's time. Modern viewers are overloaded with content, which makes attention a scarce resource. The moment a video feels slow, confusing, repetitive, or directionless, the viewer leaves. Your job as a long-form creator is not to hold attention by being louder, faster, or more dramatic—it is to create such a clear, compelling flow that your viewer never has a reason to click away. The opening thirty seconds set the tone. Retention begins with clarity: what is the video about, why should they watch, what will they gain, and how quickly can you deliver your first valuable moment? A strong intro does not need hype; it needs direction. That direction tells viewers, “This is worth your time,” and it gives the algorithm a reason to keep showing your video to others.

Once the intro hooks the viewer, your structure becomes the backbone of retention. Long-form videos require intentional planning because the viewer must always know where they are in the journey. Humans love patterns. They need sequencing. They enjoy being led through an experience rather than guessing what’s coming next. This is why the world’s most successful YouTubers use frameworks—chapters, sections, beats, story arcs, or numbered points—to give viewers mental signposts. When a video is structured, the audience feels guided and secure. When a video lacks structure, the audience gets lost and leaves. Throughout this book, you’ll learn dozens of long-form structures, but in this chapter, you must understand the foundation: every long-form video needs a beginning that promises value, a middle that delivers value, and an ending that multiplies value and drives action.

Your pacing is the next key element. Many beginners speak too slowly, include too much “setup,” or drift into tangents that dilute retention. Others go too fast, overwhelming viewers with information. Long-form pacing is not about speed—it is about *momentum*. Momentum is the feeling that something important is always coming next. Strategic pacing uses moments of energy, moments of calm, transitions that shift attention, and b-roll that gives the mind something new to process without breaking the narrative. The best creators vary their sentence length, adjust their tone, incorporate visual cues, and control the rhythm of the video much like a musician controls tempo. When pacing is done well, a 20-minute video feels like five minutes. When done poorly, even a five-minute video feels like twenty.

Beyond pacing, retention is built through *visual engagement*. Even if you film with a simple camera or smartphone, your viewer needs visual variation to stay engaged. This doesn't mean constant movement—it means strategic moments where the visual experience resets the viewer's attention. B-roll clips, overlays, graphics, zoom-ins, cutaways, screen recordings, text highlights, and changes in angle all act as visual "micro-hooks." These don't replace storytelling, but they support it, making your message easier to follow and more enjoyable to experience. Visual engagement keeps the video feeling alive. As you progress through this book, you'll learn how to use these visual tools without over-editing or distracting from your core message.

But retention does not rely solely on visuals—audio quality is equally influential, especially in long-form. A viewer can tolerate imperfect lighting or a simple background, but they will not tolerate unclear audio, echo, distortion, or volume fluctuations. Poor audio creates viewer fatigue. Excellent audio creates immersion, allowing the viewer to relax into your content for long periods. The foundation of retention is comfort. When your viewer is comfortable, they keep watching; when they're uncomfortable, they leave. This book will teach you multiple audio setups—from budget lav mics to USB microphones to smartphone-based solutions—but the principle starts here: treat audio as a primary pillar of long-form success, not an afterthought.

Another foundational skill is the ability to maintain narrative clarity throughout a long video. Long-form content requires transitions that guide the viewer from point to point without confusion. Each section must connect logically, emotionally, or contextually to the next. When viewers feel lost, they drop off, even if your content is valuable. Narrative clarity means using phrases like "Let's move into the next part," "Here's where things get interesting," "This is where most people get stuck," or "Now that you understand this, we can move to the next step." These transitions act like bridges, making the viewing experience smooth, cohesive, and predictable in the best way. Every high-retention creator uses intentional transitions. They are the invisible glue of long-form video.

The final foundational element is *viewer relationship*. Long-form video is intimate. It feels personal. Viewers spend serious time with you—they listen to your voice, watch your gestures, follow your thoughts, and form a bond that short-form videos rarely create. This relationship is what turns viewers into fans, fans into subscribers, and subscribers into customers. But the relationship must be earned through sincerity, clarity, calm authority, and consistent delivery. Audiences can sense when a creator tries too hard. They can sense when you lack conviction. They can sense when you're reading a script without understanding it. They can also sense when you genuinely care, when you respect their time, when you deliver value, and when your information comes from experience or honest intention. The creator-viewer relationship is your long-term advantage—and it starts in Chapter 1 with the mindset that every viewer matters.

This chapter establishes the pillars of long-form success: clarity, structure, pacing, audio, visuals, transitions, and relationship-building. Everything else in this book—from b-roll to editing to scripting to advanced studio setups—rests on these foundations. If you master the basics outlined here, every future video becomes easier to create, more enjoyable to watch, and more effective at generating growth, influence, and income. Long-form video is an art, but it is also a system. Master the system, and your videos will perform consistently. Master the art, and your videos will become unforgettable. The combination is what makes a true long-form creator.

"The Video That Changed Everything"

When Daniel uploaded his first YouTube video, he had no idea why almost everyone clicked away within the first thirty seconds. He had spent hours filming it, days editing it, and weeks planning the overall idea. He believed in his message. He believed he had something to offer. But the analytics told a different story. The retention graph dropped off a cliff. He stared at it in disbelief, wondering how something he worked so hard on could be dismissed so quickly. It felt unfair, confusing, and discouraging—but it also sparked something inside him. He realized that YouTube wasn't about effort. It was about understanding the viewer. And he had not done that yet.

Two months later, Daniel was sitting at his desk studying retention graphs of big creators. He watched their openings frame by frame. He analyzed how fast they spoke, how they structured their videos, how they transitioned between points, and when they added b-roll. He noticed patterns he had never seen before. They didn't waste time. They didn't ramble. They didn't guess. They guided their viewers with intention. They respected their audience's attention like a precious resource. Daniel realized that the reason his first video failed was not because he lacked passion—it was because he lacked structure. And the moment that clicked, everything changed.

He decided his next video would be different. He scripted an opening that was clear and respectful of the viewer's time. He outlined his key points in a logical flow instead of improvising. He placed b-roll markers throughout the script to add visual interest. He bought a $29 lavalier microphone to fix his audio issues. He filmed more calmly, speaking to one person—not "the internet." For the first time, Daniel felt like he wasn't recording a video; he was communicating with someone who mattered. He realized that this was the heart of long-form content: a relationship built one minute at a time.

When he uploaded the second video, he felt nervous but hopeful. The next morning, he opened YouTube Studio with the same mix of fear and excitement as before. But this time, something was different. The retention graph didn't fall off a cliff—it held. People stayed. They watched past the intro. They followed the structure. They responded to the pacing. The graph bent gently downward like a slope rather than falling like a waterfall. Daniel felt something tighten in his chest—not anxiety, but relief. He finally understood what he had been missing. YouTube wasn't just about making videos. It was about creating *experiences*. Over the next few weeks, Daniel improved rapidly. Every video he made had a clearer structure. Every transition felt smoother. His pacing became natural. His audio was consistently clean. He experimented with angles, b-roll, overlays, and subtle edits that made his videos feel alive. Viewers began leaving comments like, "I love how easy your videos are to follow," or "This felt like a conversation, not a lecture." These comments meant everything to him because they confirmed what he had learned: retention is not luck. Retention is clarity + care. And clarity plus care builds trust.

One night, a comment appeared that changed everything: "I watched the entire video without clicking away. I never do that." That sentence echoed in Daniel's mind. That was the highest compliment a long-form creator could receive. Not because it meant he was talented, but because it meant he had finally understood what viewers needed: direction, comfort, momentum, and sincerity. It wasn't about fancy gear or complicated editing. It was about respect—for the message, for the craft, and most importantly, for the viewer.

Months later, one of Daniel's videos crossed 100,000 views. Then 500,000. Then a million. The retention graphs stayed strong. His subscriber count climbed. Brands reached out. His channel became profitable. But when asked what changed everything, he didn't talk about equipment, viral ideas, or algorithm hacks. He talked about the moment he realized his first video failed for a simple reason: he hadn't guided the viewer. The day he learned to respect attention was the day his channel began to grow.

Daniel kept the retention graph of his first terrible video framed above his desk. It reminded him of where he started. It reminded him that success on YouTube begins with a simple truth: viewers stay when you give them a reason to. And that one realization—humbling, painful, and transformative—became the foundation of every long-form video he has made since.

Chapter 2

Mastering the Perfect Long-Form Video Intro

The first 30 seconds of a long-form YouTube video determine everything: your retention curve, your ranking, your watch time, your recommendations, your subscriber growth, and even your revenue. A powerful intro doesn't just "start" the video—it sets the tone, establishes direction, frames the viewer's expectations, and convinces the algorithm that your content deserves to be pushed to thousands or even millions of people. Most creators underestimate this moment, treating it like a casual warm-up instead of the most strategically important section of the entire video. In reality, your intro is the contract between you and the viewer. They must understand immediately why this video is worth watching. If they don't, they leave... and the algorithm goes with them.

The perfect intro is built around four pillars: **clarity**, **credibility**, **curiosity**, and **momentum**. Clarity tells the viewer exactly what they're about to learn or experience. Credibility reassures them that you're the right person to guide them. Curiosity activates their natural desire to stay and discover what comes next. Momentum ensures the video launches forward with energy and intention, preventing any moment of stagnation that might cause the viewer to click away. When these four elements work together, the viewer becomes invested—and once invested, they're far more likely to watch for longer periods, which is the foundation of long-form success.

Clarity is the most important element. Viewers abandon videos quickly when they are confused, overwhelmed, or unsure what the point is. Your intro must clearly answer the question: "What is this video about, and why should I care?" This is not accomplished through vague hooks like "Today we're going to talk about something really important." It is accomplished through direct statements that promise a transformation, result, or experience. Clarity creates confidence, and confidence is the gateway to trust. When viewers feel confident they're in the right place, they settle into the video rather than hovering over the exit button.

Credibility does not require bragging or listing achievements. It is established through tone, calm authority, organization, and the assurance that you know exactly where the video is going. When a creator appears centered, structured, and intentional, viewers relax. They sense expertise even without traditional credentials. Long-form success relies heavily on this unspoken confidence. You don't build credibility by telling viewers how qualified you are—you build it by demonstrating control, structure, and respect for their time from the very first line of the intro.

Curiosity is the fuel that drives attention deeper into the video. Humans are naturally wired to close loops, finish sequences, and resolve unanswered questions. Your intro must open a loop that the viewer feels compelled to close. The loop can be a mystery, a promise of value, a step-by-step process they want to follow, a transformation they want to experience, or a problem they desperately want to solve. The loop must be meaningful, relevant, and emotionally resonant. Small curiosity keeps people mildly interested; strong curiosity keeps them watching until the end.

Momentum is the rhythm that propels the viewer into the body of the video. It is created through pacing, the absence of filler words, intentional scripting, and the elimination of unnecessary details. Momentum makes the viewer feel like the video is moving forward with purpose, and that if they blink, they might miss something important. The most successful YouTubers maintain momentum through clear transitions, active language, and editing techniques that keep the viewer engaged without overwhelming them. Momentum does not mean fast—it means focused.

Once these four pillars are understood, the structure of the perfect intro becomes simple. The first sentence must immediately establish clarity. Then, within the next few lines, credibility must be felt. Soon afterward, curiosity must be activated, and finally, the intro must close with a seamless transition into the main content, preserving momentum. When followed consistently, this formula dramatically increases retention and sets your long-form videos apart from the majority of creators who simply "start talking" without intention.

In addition to these pillars, long-form intros benefit immensely from **emotional anchoring**. Emotional anchoring means connecting the topic to a feeling the viewer already has—frustration, confusion, excitement, fear of missing out, desire for improvement, or curiosity about something they've always wondered. When the viewer emotionally resonates with the opening of your video, they immediately commit more attention to it. Long-form content is not just informational; it is psychological. When a viewer feels understood, they stay. A powerful intro tells the viewer, "I get what you're going through—and I can help."

Another advanced principle for intros is **viewer identity alignment**. People watch videos that validate the identity they want to reinforce. For example, tutorials attract people who see themselves as self-improvers. Commentary attracts people who want to feel informed. Review videos attract people who want to feel smart before making decisions. Vlogs attract people who want to feel connected. When your intro subtly aligns with the viewer's identity or aspirations, you create a deeper bond from the beginning. The viewer feels seen, respected, and understood.

Finally, long-form intros must avoid the pitfalls that kill retention. Rambling kills retention. Apologizing kills retention. Long explanations about your day kill retention. Backstory kills retention unless it directly serves the viewer. Telling the viewer what you're "going to talk about today" in a generic way kills retention. Anything that delays the delivery of value kills retention. When you eliminate these habits, your intros become sharper, more powerful, and more enjoyable to watch. And once your intros become strong, every other part of your long-form videos benefits.

When you master the perfect long-form intro, everything changes. Your retention curves rise. Your watch time increases. Your videos perform better. Your subscribers trust you more. Your content becomes easier to create because your structure becomes predictable. YouTube begins to push your videos more aggressively. And most importantly, you stop losing viewers before your video even begins. The intro is not the beginning—it is the foundation. When you nail the intro, you win the video.

"Thirty Seconds That Saved the Channel"

When Maya first started her YouTube channel, she always thought intros were just a formality—a polite way to ease into the topic. She treated them casually, speaking slowly, warming up her voice, telling viewers what she *planned* to talk about instead of diving straight into value. She didn't think much of it until her analytics revealed a painful truth: almost everyone left within the first 20 to 30 seconds. It was like clockwork. Every time she uploaded a new video, the retention graph fell sharply as if the audience didn't feel any reason to stay. She wondered if her topics were wrong, if the algorithm was broken, or if she simply wasn't meant for YouTube. But deep down, she sensed the problem was in those crucial opening moments.

One afternoon, feeling frustrated, she clicked on her favorite creator's newest upload. She noticed something she had overlooked for years: he didn't waste a single second. His voice was confident from the first sentence. He didn't ramble. He didn't warm up. He didn't ease into anything. He began with a clear, compelling statement that immediately told the viewer what the video was about and why it mattered. Maya replayed the opening three times. It wasn't loud or overly dramatic—it was intentional. It was crafted. It respected the viewer's time. She felt drawn in, and the realization hit her like a spark: *This is why he succeeds. This is what I'm missing.*

That night, Maya took out a notebook and wrote down every line from the openings of five high-performing videos. She highlighted patterns she never saw before. The first sentence always promised value. The second sentence built credibility. The third opened a curiosity loop. The fourth transitioned smoothly into the main content. None of them apologized, rambled, or explained useless backstory. Their intros were tight, purposeful, and powerful. Maya realized she had been treating intros as something to get through, while top creators treated them as something to *design*. It was a turning point.

She rewrote the intro of her next video a dozen times before filming it. She practiced saying the first sentence with confidence until it felt genuine. She removed filler words. She added a curiosity hook. She rehearsed the pacing to maintain momentum. It felt weird at first, almost too direct—like she was jumping into the video too quickly. But she reminded herself that the viewer wasn't there to hear her warm up. They were there for something useful, and she was finally ready to give it to them without hesitation.

The next morning, she uploaded the video with her new intro. She watched the real-time analytics nervously, expecting the usual drop. But this time, something incredible happened: people stayed. The retention line held steady past the 30-second mark for the first time ever. It didn't fall sharply. It didn't dive. It simply... stayed. Maya gasped. She had never seen a retention graph behave like that on her channel. It felt like witnessing a miracle, but she knew it wasn't luck—it was the intro.

Over the next week, she kept checking the analytics, and every time she did, the graph still held strong. Comments began pouring in: "Great intro!", "You got straight to the point—I love that," "This hooked me from the start," and even, "I normally skip intros, but yours kept me watching." Maya felt a swell of pride and relief. She had done it. She had fixed the part of her videos that had secretly been holding her back the entire time.

As she applied the same structure to every new video, her channel began to grow faster than ever. Subscribers doubled. Watch time increased dramatically. YouTube pushed her videos to more viewers. For the first time in her creator journey, Maya felt in control. She understood what she was doing. She had unlocked a skill that most beginners never master. Her intros became her signature move, the part of her videos viewers looked forward to because they were clear, confident, and compelling.

Months later, during a livestream Q&A, someone asked her what the biggest turning point was in her channel's growth. She didn't hesitate. "The moment I learned that the intro is everything," she said. "Thirty seconds changed my channel. Thirty seconds saved it." Her audience nodded in agreement, and comments flooded the chat. They understood now. They saw the difference. And Maya knew she would never go back to the old way again.

Her intros were no longer filler—they were the spark that lit everything else. And from that day forward, every time she hit record, she remembered the moment she realized how much power a single sentence could hold.

Chapter 3

Structuring Long-Form Videos With Precision and Flow

Structure is the backbone of every high-retention long-form YouTube video. Without it, even the most valuable information collapses into confusion. Viewers don't leave because your ideas are bad—they leave because your ideas feel disorganized. Structure makes your content predictable in the best way, giving viewers mental landmarks that guide them through the journey. When the viewer subconsciously understands the flow of the video, their anxiety decreases, their attention increases, and their interest is maintained far longer than if the video feels improvised or chaotic. In long-form video, structure is not optional—it is the quiet force that keeps viewers watching beyond the first few minutes.

To build powerful structures, you need to understand how the human brain processes information during long-form consumption. Viewers cannot retain or enjoy content that jumps around without clarity. They need segmentation, sequencing, and rhythm. That's why television, documentary filmmaking, university lectures, podcasts, and bestselling books all rely on structured frameworks. YouTube is no different. The creator who masters structure becomes a creator whose videos are binge-worthy, replayed, and trusted. This chapter focuses on building those repeatable structures so every long-form video you create feels intentional, professional, and easy to watch.

One of the most reliable structures is the **Modular Breakdown Method**. In this model, the long-form video is divided into clear segments—modules—that each have a specific purpose. For a tutorial, modules may include: Step 1 (Setup), Step 2 (Explanation), Step 3 (Demonstration), Step 4 (Application), and Step 5 (Common Mistakes). For a narrative video, modules may include: The Hook, The Tension, The Discovery, The Transformation, and The Conclusion. Modular design helps the viewer feel like they are progressing through a meaningful path rather than being dragged through a stream of consciousness. Every module must be introduced clearly, delivered cleanly, and transitioned intentionally to maintain viewer confidence.

Another powerful structure is the **Problem–Promise–Process–Payoff Model**, widely used in educational and informational videos. The video begins by presenting the problem the viewer is experiencing, followed by the promise of what they will gain or understand by watching. Then comes the process: the steps, concepts, breakdowns, or demonstrations. Finally, the video ends with the payoff—the resolution, transformation, or simplified summary that delivers emotional satisfaction. This four-part structure mirrors the psychological journey viewers naturally want to experience. It creates narrative momentum while also giving the viewer a reason to continue watching until the payoff arrives. When videos follow this pattern, retention rises dramatically.

Some videos benefit from the **Layered Depth Structure**, where the creator begins with broad concepts and gradually moves into deeper or more advanced details. This structure works extremely well for educational content because it allows viewers with different knowledge levels to follow along without feeling overwhelmed. Beginners receive enough foundational context to stay engaged, while advanced viewers still gain value from the deeper layers that come later. Layered depth ensures the video appeals to a wider audience and maintains retention across varying experience levels. If you've ever watched a video that suddenly became too complex too quickly, you've experienced what happens when the structure lacks layered depth.

There is also the **Story-Driven Framework**, which leverages narrative techniques to increase retention. Humans are naturally wired for stories. When information is embedded within a narrative sequence, the viewer's brain becomes more engaged and more emotionally connected. This structure works particularly well for documentaries, personal development videos, commentary content, educational storytelling, and transformation-based videos. The structure includes a compelling character, a challenge or conflict, a journey or process, and a resolution that provides meaning or insight. Even in instructional videos, the creator can weave in micro-stories to deepen connection and enhance retention.

Transitions are the glue that holds structure together. Without strong transitions, the best structure collapses because the viewer feels mentally "dropped" between sections. A transition should give closure to the previous section while opening a curiosity loop for the next. Phrases like "Now that you understand the foundation, let's move into the part nobody talks about," or "This next step is where most people make mistakes," create directional flow. Long-form videos without transitions feel choppy and exhausting. Videos with transitions feel professional and easy to follow. Your viewers may not consciously notice transitions, but they absolutely feel them—and their retention depends on them.

Another key structural principle is **reducing cognitive load**. Cognitive load is the mental effort required to process information. When videos overwhelm viewers with too many ideas too quickly, they feel mentally tired and leave. To reduce cognitive load, break complex ideas into smaller pieces, use simple language, provide examples, and avoid introducing too many concepts at once. Structure should simplify—not complicate—the viewer's understanding. A well-structured video makes even complex topics feel clear and digestible. Reducing cognitive load is one of the most underrated skills in long-form video production.

Strong long-form structures also incorporate **strategic resets**, which are small shifts in pacing, visuals, or tone that refresh the viewer's attention. These resets may include a short b-roll moment, a quick demonstration, a screen recording, a zoom-in, or a shift in angle. Each reset acts as a micro-break for the viewer's brain, giving them a moment to reset their focus without losing engagement. These resets are essential for videos longer than eight minutes, and they become even more important for videos longer than fifteen or twenty minutes. Without resets, even the best structure can lose momentum.

Finally, every structured long-form video must end with a **completion reward**. This reward acknowledges the viewer's time investment and gives them emotional or psychological closure. The reward may be a summary, a final insight, an inspiring message, a practical takeaway, or a cliffhanger that leads them into the next video. Endings matter because they determine whether the viewer binge-watches your content, subscribes, likes, comments, or leaves your channel forever. Completion rewards create loyal viewers who keep returning because they trust that watching your videos will deliver value until the very last second.

Mastering structure is one of the greatest advantages you can have in long-form content. It turns your videos from scattered thoughts into compelling experiences. It transforms your information into a journey. It makes your viewers feel guided, understood, and supported. When your structure is strong, your content becomes stronger, your retention rises, and your creator identity becomes more defined. Structure allows creativity to flourish rather than collapse. It allows your ideas to land. It creates clarity—and clarity creates power.

"The Blueprint That Changed the Channel"

When Olivia started her YouTube channel, she believed passion would be enough. She had energy, enthusiasm, and a genuine desire to help people. But no matter how hard she worked, her videos always felt messy. She'd jump from idea to idea, lose her train of thought, and overwhelm her viewers with too much information delivered too quickly. In the comments, people said things like "Great info, but hard to follow," or "I got lost halfway through," or "This would be amazing if it was more organized." The comments didn't hurt her feelings—they confused her. She thought she *was* being organized. But clearly, viewers disagreed.

One day, a viewer left a comment that stuck with her: "Your ideas are brilliant, but the flow is chaotic." That word—chaotic—echoed in her mind. Chaos wasn't her intention. She wanted clarity, transformation, and connection. Yet chaos was what people experienced. That night, she lay awake thinking about her videos, wondering what she was missing. Why did the content in her head feel so different from the content on the screen? Why did her viewers feel overwhelmed even when she tried her best to be clear?

The breakthrough came unexpectedly when Olivia watched a documentary about architecture. The narrator explained how a building with a strong blueprint can withstand storms, pressure, and unexpected challenges. A building without a blueprint collapses under its own weight. Olivia froze. It was the same with her videos. She had been creating without a blueprint. She had been improvising, hoping clarity would magically appear. She realized that no creator—no matter how passionate—could maintain viewer attention without structure.

Inspired, she grabbed a notebook and wrote: *My videos need a blueprint.* She spent days researching long-form frameworks, studying creators who made complex topics feel simple. She discovered the power of modules, the significance of transitions, the need for pacing, and the psychological journey viewers expect from long-form content. Each discovery felt like a missing puzzle piece sliding into place. For the first time, she understood why her videos felt chaotic—not because she lacked talent, but because she lacked structure.

Her next video was the first one she had ever built using a clear framework. She used the Problem–Promise–Process–Payoff structure. She outlined each section. She wrote transitions that guided the viewer from one idea to the next. She removed unnecessary details. She added strategic resets to keep the viewer's attention steady. She rehearsed the flow until she could feel the rhythm of the video as if it were music. When she pressed record, something felt different—she felt calm. She knew where the video was going. She wasn't guessing. She was guiding.

When she uploaded it, she didn't expect miracles. But the next morning, she saw something she had never seen before: the retention graph held steady, not just for the first few minutes, but all the way through the midpoint. Comments flooded in: "This is so easy to follow," "Finally, a clear explanation," "You broke this down perfectly," and "This is your best video yet." Olivia felt tears in her eyes. Her blueprint had worked.

She repeated the process for the next video, then the next. Each time, the results grew stronger. Watch time increased. Subscribers multiplied. Her videos began appearing in suggested feeds. Fellow creators asked her how she had suddenly improved so quickly. She smiled, knowing the answer: structure. Her channel didn't grow because she got better equipment or worked harder. It grew because she finally built videos the same way an architect builds a skyscraper—with intention, depth, and a clear foundation.

Months later, Olivia looked back at her old videos and didn't feel embarrassment—she felt gratitude. Those messy, chaotic, well-intentioned videos had taught her what she needed to know. They were the stepping stones to clarity. They reminded her of how far she had come. Now, she was a creator with a blueprint. And every time she planned a video, she whispered a quiet promise to her viewers: *You will never feel lost again.*

Chapter 4

The Art of Pacing: Controlling Viewer Momentum in Long-Form Videos

Pacing is one of the most misunderstood yet influential elements of long-form YouTube content. It determines how smoothly the viewer moves through your video, how energized they feel, how long they stay, and how much mental fatigue they accumulate along the way. Many beginner creators believe pacing is simply about speaking faster or adding more cuts, but pacing is far more complex and nuanced than that. True pacing is the craft of managing attention, controlling energy, guiding emotion, and creating forward movement without overwhelming or exhausting the viewer. It is the invisible engine that drives retention. If structure is the blueprint of your long-form video, pacing is the heartbeat.

Long-form pacing begins with understanding **viewer tension cycles**. Human attention naturally rises and falls. People become highly focused during moments of novelty, clarity, or emotional connection; their attention dips during monotony, confusion, or cognitive overload. Exceptional pacing works with these attention cycles rather than against them. Instead of maintaining a constant speed, wise creators vary pacing intentionally—slowing down during complex explanations, speeding up during exciting transitions, adding visual resets at predictable intervals, and reducing cognitive load with simple summaries after intense sections. When pacing aligns with natural attention cycles, viewers subconsciously feel "pulled forward," leading to significantly higher retention.

The first major pacing tool is **sentence density**, which refers to how much information you deliver per sentence. High-density sentences can feel overwhelming, especially when stacked together. Low-density sentences may feel too slow or repetitive. The key is balance. During technical explanations, use shorter, clearer sentences with more breathing space. During storytelling or high-energy sequences, use longer, flowing sentences that build momentum. Every shift in density subtly influences the viewer's experience. When creators ignore density, their videos either feel rushed or painfully slow. When creators understand density, their content feels effortlessly engaging.

The second pacing tool is **visual variation**. Long-form viewers need visual stimulation at regular intervals to stay mentally alert. Visual variation includes b-roll sequences, text overlays, graphics, cutaways, zoom-ins, angle changes, on-screen highlights, and movement within the frame. These are not decorative; they are functional. They reset the viewer's brain. They provide micro-breaks without interrupting the narrative. They prevent visual fatigue. The mistake beginners make is either using too much variation (leading to chaos) or too little (leading to boredom). Effective pacing uses variation rhythmically, like beats in music. The goal is not constant stimulation—it is strategic stimulation.

Another central pacing principle is **verbal rhythm**. Your natural speaking cadence influences viewer comfort. Speaking too fast creates anxiety; speaking too slow creates boredom. Verbal rhythm becomes especially important in longer videos, where the viewer listens to your voice for extended periods. The most successful long-form creators treat their voice like an instrument, adjusting tone, tempo, inflection, and emphasis to match the energy of the moment. A calm tone during explanations, an enthusiastic tone during transitions, a slower tone during emotional points, and a sharper tone during key insights all create a listening experience that feels dynamic rather than monotonous.

Pacing also depends heavily on **segment length**. When your segments are too long without breaks, viewers experience attention fatigue. When segments are too short, viewers feel disoriented and unable to settle into the content. A strong long-form video rhythmically alternates between short, medium, and long segments. For example: a short 15-second hook, a medium 60-second explanation, a longer 2-minute breakdown, followed by a 10-second visual reset. This combination feels natural to viewers because it mirrors the subconscious rhythms found in conversation, storytelling, and film.

One of the most advanced pacing strategies is the use of **internal hooks**—short moments inside the video that reignite attention. Internal hooks can be: "This next part is where most people fail," or "Now here's something surprising," or "Before we move on, you need to understand this one thing," or "This is where it gets interesting." These hooks stimulate curiosity, keeping viewers mentally alert. When a creator places internal hooks at the right intervals, their retention graph dramatically improves. Internal hooks are crucial for videos greater than 10 minutes and essential for videos greater than 20.

A crucial but overlooked pacing tool is **cognitive decompression**. Every time you teach something complex, the viewer's brain gets heavier. If you immediately introduce another intense concept, the viewer becomes overloaded and quits. Cognitive decompression moments are short, intentional pauses where you simplify, summarize, or shift perspective. These decompression moments allow the viewer's brain to reset before continuing. It is similar to resting between sets in the gym—you allow recovery so the viewer can keep going. Without decompression, long-form videos feel like mental marathons. Equally important is **emotional pacing**, the art of guiding how the viewer feels throughout the experience. Emotional pacing includes excitement, calm, anticipation, curiosity, relief, tension, and satisfaction. Too much excitement exhausts the viewer. Too much calm bores them. Too much tension stresses them. Too much relief disengages them. Emotional pacing regulates the emotional arc of the video so the viewer feels like they're on a journey rather than a lecture. When creators master emotional pacing, their videos feel immersive and cinematic, even if filmed simply.

The final pacing element is **endurance awareness**—the acknowledgment that viewers who make it past certain time milestones must be guided differently. The pacing for the first minute is different from the pacing for minutes 8–12, and different from the pacing for minutes 18–25. As a viewer progresses through a long video, their attention becomes more stable but their cognitive load becomes heavier. This means pacing must become slightly simpler, smoother, and more emotionally supportive as the video continues. Many creators lose viewers toward the end not because the information is weak but because the pacing becomes too heavy too late.

Mastering pacing is what turns long-form videos into watchable experiences rather than endurance tests. When pacing is poor, even short videos feel long. When pacing is excellent, even long videos feel short. Pacing is one of the fundamental skills that separates amateur creators from professionals. It makes your videos easier to watch, more engaging, and more emotionally resonant. It improves retention more than almost any other skill. And once you master pacing, the rest of long-form creation becomes dramatically easier because you finally understand the rhythm that keeps a viewer fully immersed from beginning to end.

"When the Video Finally Flowed"

Miles had always loved creating YouTube videos, but there was one problem he couldn't seem to solve: his videos felt slow. Not boring—just slow. Viewers left after a few minutes, even when the topic was good. His friends said his content was valuable, but something about the flow felt off. In his analytics dashboard, the retention graphs always dipped early. No matter how much energy he put in, his videos felt like they dragged. He couldn't understand why. He talked clearly, he had solid information, and he even added graphics. But nothing changed the fact that people weren't staying.

One evening, frustrated after watching retention drop to 22 percent by the third minute, Miles decided to rewatch one of his own videos. This time, he didn't watch as the creator—he watched as the viewer. And suddenly, everything became clear. He realized the problem wasn't the message—it was the pacing. He paused the video at random moments and noticed long stretches where nothing changed visually. His voice stayed exactly the same. His sentences were long and heavy. He jumped from point to point without rhythm. There were moments where he spoke too slowly, followed by moments where he delivered too much at once. The experience felt uneven. For the first time, Miles understood why people left.

Determined to improve, Miles began studying creators who kept viewers watching for twenty minutes or more. He studied their delivery, their transitions, their editing choices, and their visual variety. He noticed how they used rhythmic shifts—slightly faster moments after slower ones, zoom-ins after still shots, b-roll sprinkles after heavy explanations. They weren't just talking; they were guiding attention. Their pacing felt like music, with rises and falls that kept the viewer emotionally engaged. Miles realized he had been speaking like a lecturer when he needed to speak like a storyteller.

He rewrote the script for his next video, focusing not just on what he said but on how it flowed. He added shorter sentences in complex sections. He simplified explanations. He added internal hooks every minute—small moments that woke the viewer's curiosity. He recorded multiple takes with different speaking rhythms until he found one that felt natural yet dynamic. He added b-roll markers throughout the script to ensure the video never visually stalled. For the first time in his creator life, he felt like he wasn't just sharing information—he was crafting an experience.

When he edited the video, he approached it with new eyes. He trimmed unnecessary pauses. He used subtle zoom-ins during important lines. He added brief visual resets after dense explanations. He adjusted background music to match emotional pacing. He even rearranged a few sections to create a smoother emotional arc. The edit took longer than usual, but Miles felt something he hadn't felt in months—excitement. The pacing felt right. It felt alive. He couldn't wait to see if viewers noticed.

When he published the video, he refreshed the page obsessively. Within the first hour, retention stayed high. By the end of the day, it was his best-performing video ever. For the first time, viewers made it past the midpoint—many even reached the end. Comments poured in: "This flowed perfectly," "Super easy to watch," "Great energy," "Best pacing I've seen from you." Miles felt a rush of validation. His hard work had paid off. He finally understood the secret ingredient that had been missing.

Over the next few videos, Miles kept refining his pacing. Each new upload performed better than the last. His channel grew faster. Viewers praised his delivery. He felt in control of his craft for the first time. One night, as he edited a new video, he realized something profound: pacing wasn't about being fast—it was about being intentional. It was about respecting how people absorb information, how they feel, and how their attention moves. It was the rhythm of storytelling, not the speed of speaking.

Months later, when he compared his old videos to his new ones, he smiled. The difference was staggering. The old videos felt stiff and heavy. The new videos felt smooth and dynamic. He had learned a skill that transformed his channel completely. And every time someone commented "Great pacing!" he felt a surge of gratitude for that one night when he finally understood why viewers left—and how to make them stay.

Chapter 5

Mastering B-Roll: Visual Storytelling for High-Retention Long-Form Videos

B-roll is one of the most powerful tools in long-form video production, yet it is also one of the most misunderstood. Many creators treat b-roll as decoration—extra footage layered on top of their main talking head to "make things look better." But in professional filmmaking, b-roll is never decorative. It is functional. It reinforces meaning, reduces viewer fatigue, guides attention, strengthens pacing, clarifies explanations, and dramatically improves retention. In long-form YouTube content, b-roll serves as the visual glue that keeps the viewer emotionally and mentally engaged, especially during dense sections of information or narration. When done well, the viewer barely notices the b-roll—but they feel its impact deeply.

The purpose of b-roll is simple: to give the viewer's brain something new to look at without breaking the narrative. Human attention declines when the visual environment becomes static. If the screen remains unchanged for too long, the viewer subconsciously disengages—even if the content is interesting. B-roll resets attention through variety. It activates new visual pathways. It prevents visual fatigue. It supports the story by showing rather than telling. Well-timed b-roll creates a rhythm that keeps the viewer watching longer, which is essential for long-form retention. It also makes your video feel more cinematic and more professional, which enhances viewer trust.

The most important concept in long-form b-roll is **relevance**. Every piece of b-roll must serve the message. Random footage confuses the viewer and cheapens the experience. Effective b-roll visually represents the idea you are explaining—or at minimum, enhances the emotional tone of the moment. If you're discussing a workspace setup, show clips of desks, lighting, or gear. If you're explaining mindset, show scenes that evoke energy, calmness, or creativity. If you're teaching a process, show each step being performed. The goal of relevant b-roll is alignment. Alignment between audio and visuals increases comprehension and makes the content more satisfying to consume.

Another key principle is **timing**. B-roll must appear at the right moment—never too soon, never too late. If b-roll appears too early, it steals attention from the concept you are trying to explain. If it appears too late, it feels disconnected. The best timing occurs when you reach a moment of high clarity, impact, or complexity. For example, if you're explaining a difficult concept, dropping in visual diagrams or screen recordings at the exact moment the explanation becomes heavy can dramatically improve understanding. Timing also helps pacing. Well-timed b-roll gives the audience a mental break, allowing them to recover their attention before the next section begins.

In long-form videos, b-roll should be used strategically rather than constantly. Too much b-roll creates overstimulation and weakens the viewer's connection to your face, which is essential for trust-building. Too little b-roll makes the video visually dull. The ideal balance depends on the nature of your content, but most high-retention long-form videos benefit from b-roll appearing every 20–45 seconds in some form. This doesn't mean full-screen b-roll every time; sometimes a small overlay, a zoom, or a partial visual insert is enough to refresh attention. What matters is the rhythm: b-roll must maintain the visual heartbeat of the video.

A powerful concept in b-roll strategy is **emotional reinforcement**. Not all b-roll is informational. Some b-roll exists to enhance the mood, energy, or atmosphere of the moment. For example, if you are discussing growth, ambition, or transformation, b-roll of movement—walking, typing, creating, traveling—can subconsciously elevate the viewer's internal state. If you're sharing something reflective or vulnerable, slower b-roll can deepen emotional resonance.

Emotional reinforcement helps the viewer feel what you want them to feel, making the message more impactful and memorable.

For educational or tutorial-style videos, **demonstration b-roll** is critical. Demonstration b-roll shows the viewer exactly what you are explaining. If you're teaching editing, this includes screen recordings. If you're showing camera settings, this includes shots of the gear. If you're explaining processes, show each step clearly. Demonstration b-roll prevents confusion and reduces cognitive load because the viewer sees what you mean instead of trying to visualize it. This type of b-roll dramatically increases retention because viewers stay longer when they understand clearly.

One advanced b-roll technique involves **contrast resets**—moments where the b-roll shifts drastically in tone, angle, color, or content to shock the viewer's attention back into focus. Contrast resets should be used sparingly but strategically, especially during longer videos where viewers may drift mentally. A well-placed reset can bring back a drifting viewer without them realizing why they suddenly became alert again. These resets must be purposeful—they should align with an important point, a moment of emotional transition, or a shift in the direction of the narrative.

A core principle of long-form b-roll strategy is **simplicity over complication**. Amateur creators often overthink b-roll: they believe they need cinematic shots, advanced lighting, or expensive equipment. In reality, some of the best long-form b-roll is extremely simple. Screen recordings, simple cutaways of hands working, typing on a computer, adjusting a camera, eating breakfast, walking outside, or even basic stock footage can be highly effective. What matters is relevance, rhythm, and placement—not production value. B-roll is not a test of your camera skills; it is a tool for attention control.

Another essential component is **consistency**. Consistent b-roll style—consistent color grading, consistent movement, consistent transitions—creates cohesion. If your b-roll looks random or stylistically scattered, the viewer feels subconsciously disoriented. Cohesion creates comfort, and comfort extends retention. Consistency does not mean repeating the same clips; it means maintaining a unified visual language.

Finally, long-form videos must use **b-roll as a pacing partner**. Pacing and b-roll are inseparable. Pacing tells you when b-roll is needed. B-roll supports the pacing. If a section becomes heavy, b-roll softens it. If a section becomes slow, b-roll energizes it. If a section becomes overwhelming, b-roll simplifies it. When these systems work together, the viewer feels supported from beginning to end. This synergy transforms your videos from simply informative to truly immersive.

Masterful b-roll use is one of the highest-leverage skills in long-form YouTube creation. It improves retention, strengthens messaging, deepens emotional impact, clarifies communication, enhances pacing, and keeps viewers watching long after they normally would have clicked away. Once you understand how b-roll supports your storytelling, you will never see it as "extra footage" again—you will see it as the visual architecture that makes your videos not just watchable, but memorable.

"The Day the Video Came Alive"

Before Daniel ever learned proper b-roll techniques, his videos always felt flat. Not empty—just flat. The information was good, the delivery was solid, and the audio was clean, but something was missing. Viewers stayed for a few minutes and then drifted away. Even Daniel could feel it when he rewatched his work: the videos lacked movement. They lacked texture. They lacked visual life. They were technically correct but emotionally empty. And every time he looked at the retention graph, he saw the same painful truth—people were leaving because the video didn't feel alive.

One afternoon, while researching filmmaking techniques, Daniel stumbled upon a behind-the-scenes breakdown of a documentary series. The director said something that hit him harder than he expected: "A story isn't told with images—it's told with the *right* images at the *right* moments." Daniel replayed that sentence three times. The right images at the right moments. It echoed in his mind like a revelation. He realized his videos didn't lack images—they lacked the right images. His b-roll wasn't reinforcing anything. It was random, almost decorative. He wasn't guiding the viewer—he was filling space.

Determined to fix this, Daniel began studying b-roll like a science. He watched creators who incorporated b-roll naturally and noticed patterns he had never seen before. When they explained something complex, they used simple cutaways to clarify it. When they shared stories, they used emotional b-roll that matched the feeling of the moment. When they needed a reset, they used movement-based b-roll to restore energy. Every choice was intentional. Every clip served a purpose. Daniel realized that b-roll wasn't just a visual break—it was part of the storytelling.

The next day, he decided to overhaul his approach entirely. He wrote his script but left intentional spaces for b-roll notes. Instead of collecting footage after filming, he planned it beforehand. He asked himself questions: "What should the viewer *see* at this moment? What emotion needs support right now? Would this concept be clearer if I showed it instead of saying it?" For the first time, he felt like he wasn't just shooting video—he was crafting an experience. When he filmed, he captured simple b-roll: his hands typing, flipping through a notebook, adjusting his camera, walking outside, preparing his workspace, highlighting notes. Nothing cinematic. Nothing complex. Just real moments that matched his narrative. Then he gathered a few stock clips that reinforced emotions and concepts he couldn't film easily. It was the first time his b-roll had structure. The first time it had intention. He didn't need Hollywood shots—he needed meaningful ones.

Editing the video felt different this time. Instead of sprinkling footage randomly, he matched each clip to the exact sentence it supported. He added b-roll to break up heavy explanations. He added emotional clips during reflective moments. He added movement during transitions. As he watched the rough cut, something incredible happened—the video felt alive. It had rhythm. It had energy. It had warmth. It didn't feel like a lecture—it felt like a journey.

When he uploaded the video, he expected moderate improvement, maybe a slight increase in retention. But what happened shocked him. Viewers stayed. They watched longer.

They commented about how "smooth" and "enjoyable" the video felt. Someone even wrote, "I didn't expect to watch the whole thing—but I did." Tears filled Daniel's eyes. That comment meant everything. For the first time in his creator journey, the video didn't feel flat. It breathed.

Over the following weeks, Daniel refined his technique. His videos became more textured, more dynamic, more emotionally resonant. His channel grew faster. His retention graphs smoothed out. He stopped worrying about viewers leaving because he now understood how to hold their attention visually. The breakthrough wasn't expensive gear—it was intentional storytelling. And every time he planned new b-roll, he remembered the director's words: the right images at the right moments.

The day his video came alive was the day his channel truly began.

Chapter 6

Mastering Audio: The Hidden Foundation of Long-Form Video Success

Audio quality is the most underestimated factor in long-form YouTube content, yet it is the single most influential element in determining whether a viewer stays or leaves. Viewers can tolerate imperfect lighting, simple backgrounds, or basic cameras, but they will *never* tolerate bad audio. Harsh echoes, background noise, inconsistent volume, muffled voices, or piercing frequencies create instant discomfort, and discomfort destroys retention. When the viewer feels strained, annoyed, or fatigued by the audio, they click away long before they absorb your message. In long-form video—where viewers may spend 10, 20, or even 45 minutes with you—audio is not optional. It is the foundation of immersion, trust, and long-term viewer satisfaction.

Audio quality influences viewer psychology more deeply than most creators realize. Clean audio makes the viewer feel safe, comfortable, and relaxed. When your voice is warm, clear, and stable, the viewer subconsciously feels like they can trust you. It creates the sensation of a personal conversation or a guided experience rather than a harsh broadcast. Poor audio, on the other hand, causes the viewer to tense their jaw, narrow their eyes, and brace themselves mentally. This tension increases cognitive load and reduces emotional openness. Even if the information is excellent, the viewer's body reacts negatively. Great audio lowers barriers. Bad audio raises them.

The first key principle of long-form audio is **proximity**. Microphones sound drastically better when placed close to the speaker. Distance introduces echo, muddiness, and volume dips. Whether you use a lavalier mic, a shotgun mic, or a USB condenser, the microphone must be positioned correctly to capture vocal richness while minimizing environmental interference. Many beginners rely on camera-mounted mics or smartphone mics too far from their mouth. This creates thin, distant, echoing audio that feels unprofessional. Close-mic techniques, even with inexpensive gear, instantly elevate your sound to professional levels.

The second principle is **environment control**. Great audio does not come from expensive equipment—it comes from the right space. Hard surfaces reflect sound, causing echo and reverb. Soft surfaces absorb sound, creating warmth and clarity. Curtains, rugs, clothing, soft furniture, blankets, and even pillows placed strategically off-camera can dramatically improve acoustics. A small room often sounds better than a large open one. The goal is to reduce reflections and create an intimate, controlled environment where your voice is the star. Without controlling your space, even high-end microphones cannot produce clean audio.

Another crucial concept is **noise management**. Background noise—air conditioners, refrigerators, traffic, computer fans, kids playing, or dogs barking—becomes even more distracting in long-form videos because viewers are exposed to it for extended periods. Noise deepens fatigue. It makes the brain work harder to focus on your voice. Eliminate noise sources when possible, record at quieter times of day, and use microphones with directional pickup patterns that isolate sound. Noise reduction tools in editing software help, but they cannot rescue severely noisy recordings. Clean audio begins at the source, not in post-production.

Consistency is another cornerstone of professional long-form audio. Volume fluctuations, tonal shifts, and microphone bumps disrupt viewer immersion. Your voice must remain stable throughout the entire video. This requires consistent microphone placement, consistent speaking distance, consistent posture, and consistent room conditions. If your audio quality fluctuates, the viewer becomes aware of the technical process instead of the content. Immersion breaks.

Retention drops. Great long-form audio feels invisible. It simply *is*. The viewer should never think about it.

The next core principle is **vocal delivery**. Your microphone amplifies not just your words but your emotional presence. Warmth, clarity, intention, and confidence transmit through your voice. Viewers can hear tension, hesitation, insecurity, excitement, sincerity, and fatigue. This is why vocal control matters. Speaking too quickly overwhelms the viewer; speaking too slowly bores them. Speaking too softly makes them strain; speaking too loudly feels abrasive. The best long-form delivery feels natural and rhythmic, with subtle variations in tone that match the content's emotional flow. Your voice becomes part of the storytelling.

Another advanced audio strategy involves **layered sound design**. While many creators rely entirely on voice alone, subtle background music can significantly improve viewer immersion when used carefully. Music must be quiet, non-intrusive, and tonally aligned with the content. It should enhance mood, not compete with your voice. Transitions between segments can also benefit from brief sound cues, which act as auditory resets. These resets help maintain pacing and attention. However, sound design must remain purposeful. Overuse of effects or high-volume music overwhelms the viewer. Restraint is the key.

Editing plays a major role in achieving professional audio. Equalization (EQ) enhances vocal warmth and clarity by adjusting frequencies. Compression stabilizes volume levels so quiet parts aren't too quiet and loud parts aren't too loud. Limiting prevents peaks from clipping. Noise reduction removes minor background hums or static. These are not advanced technical luxuries—they are essential tools. Even basic software includes these functions. Learning simple EQ and compression techniques instantly elevates your audio to a higher standard. It is a small investment of time with massive returns in viewer satisfaction and retention.

Monitoring your audio properly is crucial as well. Many creators make the mistake of editing their videos using laptop speakers or cheap earbuds, which hide imperfections. Professional creators monitor audio through reliable headphones or studio monitors so they can catch issues early. What sounds "fine" on weak speakers may sound unpleasant or inconsistent on good headphones. Because viewers watch videos on a wide range of devices, your audio must hold up under all listening conditions. Testing through multiple devices helps ensure consistency and comfort for everyone.

Finally, long-form YouTube audio must reflect **emotional trust-building**. Your voice is the viewer's companion throughout the entire experience. It is the element they connect to most deeply. Warm, clean audio makes the viewer feel like you are right there with them—guiding, teaching, sharing, supporting. Bad audio creates distance, while great audio creates intimacy. When your voice feels like a safe presence, viewers stay longer, return more often, and form stronger loyalty to your channel. Audio is not just sound—it is connection.

Mastering long-form audio unlocks a new level of professionalism, comfort, and viewer engagement. It reduces fatigue, increases retention, strengthens emotional resonance, and elevates your content far beyond what visuals alone can achieve. When you understand how deeply audio influences the viewer's body and mind, you begin to treat it as the foundational layer of your video—not an accessory. Your voice becomes the anchor. And once your audio becomes truly excellent, your videos feel more trustworthy, more enjoyable, and more immersive than ever before.

"The Night the Silence Spoke"

A year into building his YouTube channel, Lucas couldn't understand why viewers kept leaving. His visuals were excellent. His lighting looked professional. His editing was clean. He invested in a good camera, learned color grading, and even mastered b-roll. But still, the retention graphs told the same painful story: viewers dropped off early, drifted away slowly, or clicked away during moments where nothing major happened on screen. For months, Lucas blamed the algorithm, the niche, and even himself. But one night, all of that changed because of a moment of silence.

It was late. Lucas was editing his newest video when he noticed a slight hum in the background during one sentence. Curious, he isolated the audio. He expected the hum to be negligible. Instead, he heard something shocking—his voice sounded thin, echoing, and distant. The hum was just one part of the problem. The real issue was the room itself. His voice bounced off the walls. It sounded cold and metallic. There were faint tapping noises, shifts in chair movement, and air conditioning vibrations he never noticed before. The silence wasn't silent at all; it was noisy, uncomfortable, and unpleasant. And suddenly, everything made sense.

Lucas rewatched old videos with fresh ears. He realized what he had been blind to for so long: his audio was hurting the viewer. The echo made it hard to listen for long periods. The background sounds created subconscious irritation. The inconsistency in his tone made the viewer feel unstable. His voice lacked warmth, clarity, and presence. No wonder people left. They weren't abandoning the content—they were escaping the audio.

For the first time in his creator journey, Lucas understood that sound mattered more than almost anything else. The next morning, he went into his room and listened. Really listened. He clapped his hands and heard reflections. He whispered and heard reverb. He closed the door and realized the AC hum was louder than he thought. He began stacking pillows behind the microphone, placing blankets on the walls, closing curtains, and covering his desk with a soft cloth. The room felt different. Quieter. Warmer. More controlled. He didn't buy new gear. He simply shaped the environment to support his voice.

When he sat down to record again, he brought the microphone closer than ever before. He adjusted his posture. He slowed his breathing. He spoke with intention, not performance. When he played the audio back, his eyes widened. The difference was unbelievable. His voice sounded full, close, intimate—as if he were speaking directly to the viewer rather than across the room. For the first time, he felt emotionally connected to his own sound. It wasn't perfect, but it was real. It was comfortable.

He applied EQ and compression gently. He removed a low hum. He stabilized the volume. As he listened to the edited audio, he felt something he had never felt before while working on YouTube—a sense of presence. The voice coming out of the speakers felt like a person the viewer could trust. A companion. A guide. A real human being. When he merged the audio with the visuals, the entire video felt transformed. It wasn't a video anymore—it was an experience.

When Lucas uploaded the new video, he wasn't sure what would happen. But within the first hour, comments started appearing: "Your voice sounds amazing now," "This is the most relaxing video you've made," "I actually stayed for the whole thing," "Finally—your content matches your production quality," and even, "I didn't know audio could make such a difference." His retention graph, normally full of dips, held steady. It was the highest watch time he had ever received.

Over the next few weeks, Lucas rebuilt his recording environment completely. He created a small vocal corner. He invested in a simple but effective microphone upgrade. He practiced speaking with clarity and warmth. His videos became easier to watch. Viewers stayed longer. His channel grew faster. He felt more confident, more connected, and more skilled. His voice was no longer an obstacle—it was an asset.

Looking back months later, Lucas realized it all began with that moment of silence—the night he finally heard what his viewers had been hearing all along. It was the night he understood that long-form video is not just about what people see—it's about what they feel when they hear you. And once he mastered his audio, everything else finally fell into place.

Chapter 7

On-Camera Presence: Becoming a Confident, Compelling Long-Form Creator

On-camera presence is one of the most transformative skills a long-form creator can develop, yet it is also one of the most misunderstood. Many people believe presence is something you're born with—natural charisma, effortless confidence, the ability to speak fluidly and appear comfortable on screen. But presence is not innate; it is learned. It is a combination of psychological mastery, emotional regulation, vocal control, body language, authenticity, and the ability to make the viewer feel seen and valued. Long-form videos succeed when the viewer connects with you. They stay because you feel trustworthy, calm, knowledgeable, and human. Presence is not about performing—it is about aligning your internal state with your external communication so the viewer feels guided, not pressured.

The first core principle of on-camera presence is **intention**. Viewers can instantly sense when you are speaking without purpose. Rambling, filler words, and uncertainty create tension. Tension breaks connection. Intention means you know why you're speaking, where the video is going, and how your message will help the viewer. When you speak with intention, your energy stabilizes. You sound clearer. You appear more grounded. You choose words more carefully. Intention transforms you from a person talking into a person teaching, guiding, and supporting. Long-form audiences gravitate toward creators who speak with meaning rather than noise.

The second principle is **authentic emotional grounding**. Long-form viewers can hear and see everything: hesitation, nervousness, doubt, excitement, sincerity, or insecurity. You cannot hide your emotional state in long-form video—your voice, face, micro-expressions, and breathing patterns reveal it instantly. That's why presence begins before you hit record. You must regulate your emotional baseline. Calm yourself. Slow your breathing. Clear your mind. Release tension in your shoulders, jaw, and hands. Viewers feel the emotions behind your words even when they cannot articulate why. Emotional grounding makes your presence warm, stable, and trustworthy.

Another essential principle is **vocal presence**. The voice is the most intimate and direct connection you have with your viewer. Vocal presence is not about sounding dramatic—it is about sounding intentional, relaxed, confident, and varied.

Long-form videos require dynamic vocal delivery to maintain attention. Slight changes in tone, pacing, emphasis, and rhythm prevent monotony and create emotional texture. A viewer listening to your voice for twenty minutes must feel guided by tone just as much as by content. Great on-camera presence begins with listening to your own voice and shaping it intentionally to reflect clarity, empathy, authority, and approachability.

Body language also shapes presence. Your posture, gestures, eye contact, and facial expressions all communicate meaning. Good presence does not require exaggerated gestures or high-energy movement. It requires alignment. Your gestures should match your words. Your posture should reflect confidence without rigidity. Your facial expressions should convey sincerity, not performance. When your body communicates the same message as your words, the viewer feels coherence. Coherence is one of the deepest forms of trust-building. When your body and voice contradict each other, viewers may not consciously know why, but they sense something is off.

Eye contact is the psychological core of connection. In long-form video, eye contact is created by looking directly into the lens—not above it, not beside it, not down at yourself. Looking into the lens simulates looking directly into the viewer's eyes. It communicates attentiveness, care, honesty, and presence. Beginners often avoid eye contact because it feels unnatural or intimidating. But consistent lens connection transforms your on-camera presence immediately. It turns a monologue into a conversation. It pulls the viewer into the moment. It makes them feel like you are speaking to them, not an invisible crowd.

One of the most powerful yet overlooked factors in presence is **relational energy**—the energy you feel toward your viewer. If you imagine you are speaking to a harsh critic, your body tenses, your voice tightens, and your energy becomes defensive. If you imagine you are speaking to a supportive friend, your voice softens, your tone warms, and your body becomes more open. Long-form creators with powerful presence cultivate a sense of connection with the viewer. They imagine the viewer as someone they want to help, not impress. This shift in relational energy changes everything. It reduces nervousness, increases clarity, and enhances authenticity.

Presence also depends on **clarity of message**. When you know exactly what you are saying, your delivery becomes smoother. When you are unsure, the viewer feels your uncertainty. That's why outlines, scripts, and intentional planning are essential. You do not need to memorize every word, but you must understand every idea. Long-form creators with strong presence speak from structure, not improvisation. They allow their natural personality to flow within the boundaries of a clear framework. This balance creates confidence and calmness. Another advanced presence skill is **emotional pacing**. Emotional pacing is your ability to guide the viewer through shifting emotions—curiosity, excitement, reflection, tension, relief—using your voice and expressions. When your emotional pacing is flat, the viewer disconnects because their emotional system receives no stimulation. When emotional pacing is exaggerated, it feels forced or fake. True emotional pacing emerges from sincerity. You share excitement when it is genuinely exciting. You slow down when discussing something meaningful. You speak more intensely during moments of insight. This natural variation enhances connection without manipulation.

A major blocker to presence is **self-consciousness**. When creators focus on themselves—how they look, how they sound, whether they're doing well—they disconnect from the viewer. Presence requires shifting attention away from yourself and toward the viewer's experience. Ask yourself: What does the viewer need right now? How can I make this moment clearer? What tone helps them feel comfortable? What expression makes the message land? When your focus shifts from internal performance to external service, your presence becomes stronger. You stop performing and start connecting.

Finally, long-form on-camera presence is built through **repetition and refinement**. No one becomes natural on camera instantly. Every great creator started awkward, stiff, nervous, or overly rehearsed. Presence grows by recording often, reviewing often, adjusting often, and learning how your energy translates through the screen. The camera amplifies everything—your tension, your warmth, your confusion, your confidence. Over time, you learn how to show up with a presence that makes viewers feel safe, engaged, and connected. This is one of the highest forms of creator mastery.

On-camera presence is not about being perfect—it is about being present. It is about learning to bring your most grounded, clear, and connected version of yourself to every video. When you master on-camera presence, your long-form content becomes more compelling, more enjoyable, and more emotionally resonant. Viewers stay longer because they feel like they're spending time with someone they trust. Presence is the difference between a video that teaches information and a video that transforms the viewer's experience. It is the heart of long-form content.

"The Moment the Camera Stopped Feeling Like a Camera"

When Sofia first started filming YouTube videos, she dreaded the moment she had to press record. She would sit in front of the camera, adjust her posture, fix her hair, take a deep breath, and then freeze. The red light came on, and suddenly she became a different person—stiff, formal, and overly cautious. She heard her own voice sounding higher than normal, her smile looked forced, and her sentences came out fragmented as if she were trying too hard to get everything perfect. The more she filmed, the more she felt like the camera was judging her. And in the analytics, the results showed it. Viewers left early. Comments said she seemed nervous or distant. She felt invisible inside her own videos.

One evening, after another frustrating recording session, Sofia slumped on her couch and replayed her footage. She didn't watch it for content—she watched it for presence. And what she saw broke her heart a little. She didn't see herself at all. She saw someone pretending. Someone performing. Someone trying to be confident instead of *feeling* confident. Her voice sounded tight. Her eyes darted away from the lens. Her shoulders were tense. She realized that the camera hadn't stolen her presence—her fear had. She had become so focused on being perfect that she forgot to be real.

The next morning, she made a decision. Before she tried to improve her delivery, she needed to improve her emotional state. She sat in silence for five minutes, breathing deeply and calming her body. She reminded herself why she started creating videos—to help people, to share her knowledge, to connect. When she sat down to film again, she didn't launch into the script immediately. Instead, she imagined a real person on the other side of the camera—someone who genuinely needed her guidance. She softened her expression. Her shoulders relaxed. And for the first time, she felt warmth instead of fear.

She pressed record. But this time was different. Her voice felt grounded. Her smile felt real. She looked into the lens and imagined speaking to a close friend. She didn't rush. She didn't force anything. She simply spoke. When she finished, she didn't feel exhausted—she felt relieved. Curious, she played the footage back. Her jaw dropped. It wasn't perfect, but it was human. Her presence felt natural, her voice calm, her expressions genuine. It was the first time she recognized herself in a video.

Inspired, Sofia dove deeper into understanding on-camera presence. She studied creators with strong presence and noticed patterns: they didn't perform—they connected. They didn't rush—they grounded. They didn't stare at themselves—they looked through the lens as if the viewer mattered. She practiced speaking with intention, modulating her voice, using her hands naturally, and holding eye contact with the lens. She learned to shift her focus from internal anxiety to external service. Each recording session felt easier.

When she published her next video, she wasn't sure what would happen. But within hours, the comments poured in: "You seem so confident now," "This version of you feels so genuine," "I felt like you were talking directly to me," and "Your presence is so calming." Sofia felt tears fill her eyes. For the first time, people weren't commenting on her information—they were commenting on *her*. Her presence. Her connection. Her humanity.

Each new video built on that foundation. Sofia learned to warm up her voice, relax her body, and enter a state of grounded intention before filming. She stopped pretending and started showing up as her real self. Her retention graphs improved. Her subscribers grew. But the most important change was internal—she no longer felt afraid of the camera. She felt comfortable, almost peaceful. The camera stopped being a judge. It became a bridge.

Months later, during a livestream, someone asked her, "When did you finally feel confident on camera?" Sofia smiled softly and said, "The moment the camera stopped feeling like a camera—when I stopped performing and started connecting." The viewers filled the chat with hearts, and she realized something profound: presence wasn't something she achieved. It was something she allowed.

And from that day forward, every time she saw the red recording light, she didn't freeze—she opened up.

Chapter 8

Visual Effects, Transitions & Motion: Elevating Long-Form Videos With Creative Style

Visual effects, transitions, and motion design are the creative tools that transform long-form YouTube videos from simple recordings into memorable, high-retention visual experiences. While storytelling and structure form the foundation of your content, visual effects add personality, energy, clarity, and rhythm. When used strategically, they can strengthen viewer engagement, emphasize key points, guide attention, and maintain momentum. When used excessively or without intention, they can overwhelm the viewer, create distraction fatigue, and diminish trust. The goal of this chapter is to help you master the balance—using visual effects as thoughtful enhancements rather than flashy noise.

The first principle of long-form visual design is **functional creativity**. Visual effects must serve a purpose. In professional-level content, every movement and transition guides the viewer's attention, clarifies information, or supports pacing. Effects must help the story, not pull the viewer out of it. A simple zoom-in can reinforce a key insight. A subtle highlight behind text can improve readability. A smooth transition between sections can ensure pacing flows naturally. Creativity is not about volume; it is about intention. If an effect doesn't enhance clarity, emotion, or momentum, it doesn't belong.

The second principle is **subtlety over spectacle**. Many beginner creators assume visual effects must be bold, dramatic, or constantly in motion. But long-form video thrives on calm, controlled movement. Subtle animations preserve viewer comfort and avoid overwhelming the senses. Light zooms, slow pans, gentle fades, minimal transitions, or clean motion graphics often outperform exaggerated spins, flips, explosions, or rapid cuts. Viewers remain focused on your message rather than the effect. Your goal is polish, not noise. When effects are subtle, the viewer feels the improvement without consciously noticing it.

A major component of visual design in long-form content is **directional attention**. Visual effects should guide the viewer's eyes toward what matters most. If you are emphasizing a phrase, a simple text animation helps the viewer absorb the idea. If you are presenting a process, animated arrows or highlights can direct attention to crucial steps. If you are showing screen recordings, cursor tracking or motion highlights can make navigation easier to follow.

Directional effects reduce cognitive load and help the viewer stay aligned with your explanations. Every effect should point the viewer somewhere, not distract them.

Another essential principle is **rhythmic transitions**. Transitions create flow between ideas, segments, or emotional beats. A good transition feels invisible—it simply carries the viewer from one moment to the next without friction. Hard cuts work well for rapid pacing. Soft fades work for reflective or emotional content. Motion transitions such as push, slide, or whip effects add energy but must remain clean and consistent. The best long-form transitions follow the flow of the narrative rather than interrupt it. They help create an experience where the viewer glides effortlessly through long sections of content without feeling the length.

Long-form creators also benefit from mastering **kinetic typography**, which is animated text designed to visually reinforce spoken dialogue. When used intentionally, kinetic text strengthens retention by creating visual anchors around important ideas. It also breaks monotony and adds dynamic engagement. However, it must be used sparingly. Too much animated text clutters the screen and exhausts the viewer. Kinetic typography is most effective when highlighting key words, definitions, emotional beats, or actionable steps. It serves as a visual drumbeat aligning the viewer's eyes with your voice. Another advanced visual technique is **supplementary motion graphics**, which can include charts, diagrams, icons, overlays, or animated illustrations. These are especially valuable in educational content or analytical breakdowns. Motion graphics simplify complex topics, turning abstract ideas into understandable visuals. When a viewer sees a moving diagram rather than hearing a static explanation, comprehension rises dramatically. The key is simplicity. Motion graphics must make the video easier—not more complicated—to follow. Clean lines, minimal color palettes, and slow movement help maintain elegance and clarity.

A powerful form of visual enhancement is **camera motion**—either real or simulated. Real camera motion involves physically moving your camera: sliding, panning, rotating, or dollying to create dynamic shots. Simulated motion includes digital zooms or slight repositioning during editing. These small movements help maintain visual energy, especially during long monologues or intense explanations. The key is subtlety. Tiny, almost imperceptible movements feel cinematic and professional. Fast or abrupt movements feel amateur and jarring. Long-form viewers prefer gentle motion that feels comforting, not chaotic.

Alongside camera motion, **b-roll transitions** play a major role in long-form pacing. Using b-roll as a bridge between ideas creates emotional resets and prevents visual stagnation. B-roll can fade into the main clip, slide across the screen, or appear as a brief overlay. These transitions make the video feel richer and more textured without distracting from the message. The rhythm of alternating between talking head and b-roll maintains viewer comfort and engagement.

Another key component is **environmental motion**, which includes small background movements—like lights subtly shifting, a monitor glowing, a plant moving slightly, or soft ambient animations. These micro-movements make your set feel alive without distracting the viewer. They also create depth and atmosphere, contributing to your brand's visual identity. Long-form content benefits immensely from environments that feel warm and visually intentional.

Next is **tonal consistency**, which ensures that all visual effects follow the same style, color palette, speed, and mood. Inconsistent effects create subconscious discomfort, making the video feel scattered or unprofessional. Tonal consistency makes the video feel cohesive even if a variety of effects and transitions are used. Your goal is a unified visual language that supports the viewer's emotional experience from beginning to end.

Finally, visual effects must support **emotional resonance**. Motion, transitions, and effects can increase excitement, create anticipation, deepen reflection, or emphasize transformation. Emotionally aligned visuals amplify the feeling behind your words, creating a more immersive experience. Emotion drives retention. When viewers feel something, they stay longer. Visual effects are one of the subtle tools that help emotional beats land more powerfully.

Mastering visual effects, transitions, and motion design elevates your long-form videos into cinematic, memorable experiences. These tools are not about adding "flash"—they are about enhancing clarity, guiding attention, supporting emotion, and maintaining momentum. When used with intention, they transform your content from informative to captivating. Long-form viewers crave comfort, clarity, and creativity. Visual design gives them all three. And once you master these techniques, your videos will not just be watched—they will be remembered.

"The Edit That Felt Like Magic"

Elias loved filming videos, but editing always felt like a battle. He could record for hours, but when he sat down in front of the timeline, everything looked dull and lifeless. His cuts were clean, his audio crisp, his script solid—but the videos lacked pulse. They felt flat. Safe. Predictable. Whenever he compared his content to that of the creators he admired, he noticed something he couldn't replicate: their videos felt alive. Even when they weren't doing anything extraordinary, the editing had a magic that pulled him forward. He couldn't name it, but he felt it.

One frustrated evening, Elias stayed up late rewatching a creator whose videos always mesmerized him. As he scrubbed through the timeline, he slowed the video to quarter speed. Suddenly, the magic revealed itself. Tiny zooms. Soft text animations. Smooth fades. A gentle push transition when the tone shifted. A subtle highlight around a key phrase. A small movement in the background. Nothing aggressive. Nothing flashy. Just a series of subtle choices that created motion, clarity, and rhythm. Elias felt his breath catch. He whispered to himself, "It's the effects. They're invisible, but they make all the difference."

The next morning, he opened his editing software with a new mission: to make his video feel alive, not loud. He experimented with micro-zooms, barely noticeable but powerful. He added a soft fade when shifting from personal storytelling to a technical explanation. He used gentle kinetic text to emphasize important words. He layered in an animated icon to illustrate a concept. He inserted slow b-roll transitions to support pacing. None of it was dramatic. All of it was intentional. For the first time, editing didn't feel like assembly—it felt like craftsmanship. As the video came together, something inside him shifted. He watched a rough section and felt that strange sensation again—the feeling of being pulled forward, the feeling he'd admired in others. The video had rhythm now. The motion matched the emotion. The visuals guided his eyes without distraction. It felt like magic because it was cohesive, graceful, and alive. His heart raced as he played the sequence again and again, amazed at how subtle changes transformed the entire experience.

When Elias uploaded the final video, he didn't expect an explosion, but he hoped viewers would feel what he felt. Within hours, comments began pouring in: "Your editing is leveling up," "This flowed so smoothly," "Your videos are becoming more cinematic," "This is your best work yet." One comment stood out most: "I didn't realize why, but this video just felt... good." Elias leaned back in his chair, smiling deeply. That was the confirmation he needed. The magic wasn't in big effects—it was in effects the viewer didn't even notice.

Over the next month, Elias refined his visual approach. He learned restraint, consistency, and intentionality. He discovered how to highlight emotion through transitions and how to use effects to support—not overshadow—the message. He explored motion graphics that simplified complex ideas.

He learned to treat every visual element like a brushstroke in a painting rather than a decoration. Each new video felt richer than the last.

Eventually, viewers began to comment not just on the editing but on how the videos made them feel. Calm. Focused. Inspired. Immersed. Elias realized that visual effects were not tools—they were a language. A language that allowed him to communicate emotion, rhythm, and energy without saying a word. The edit that once frustrated him became the edit that defined him.

Months later, during a collaboration, another creator asked him, "What changed? Your videos feel completely different now." Elias laughed softly and replied, "I stopped trying to make them look fancy. I started trying to make them *feel* right." And in that moment, he knew he had crossed an invisible threshold. He was no longer just recording videos. He was creating experiences.

The edit had finally become magic—but only because he learned how to make the magic serve the story.

Chapter 9

Content Planning, Batching & Repurposing: Building a Sustainable Long-Form Production System

Long-form YouTube success doesn't come from creating one great video. It comes from creating great videos consistently. Consistency is the engine of momentum, and momentum is the engine of growth. But consistency doesn't happen by accident—it is built through planning, batching, and strategic repurposing. Without a system, creators burn out quickly. With a system, creators scale effortlessly. Content planning transforms creativity from an unpredictable burst into a reliable process. This chapter teaches you the exact mindset and workflow needed to create long-form content week after week without stress, burnout, or chaos.

The first principle of long-form content planning is **predictability**. Long-form videos require more time, more energy, and more mental focus than short-form content. Without structure, creators get stuck in reaction mode—constantly scrambling to come up with ideas, script videos, film content, and edit everything on time. Predictability means building a system that removes guesswork. It means knowing what you will create before you create it. When you eliminate uncertainty, creativity flows more naturally because your mind has a clear destination. The planning process reduces anxiety and gives you creative stability.

The second principle is **content categories**. Every long-form creator must identify three to five content categories that define their channel. Categories create consistency, strengthen your niche identity, and make brainstorming easier. For example, a filmmaking creator might have categories such as tutorials, gear reviews, creative techniques, and storytelling breakdowns. Categories give shape to your creative identity. Without them, your channel drifts, confusing both the viewer and the algorithm. Categories guide your long-form strategy so each video reinforces your core message.

Next is **topic sequencing**, which ensures your long-form content builds logically over time. Sequencing means you don't choose random topics—you organize them like chapters in a book. One video prepares the viewer for the next. One skill sets the foundation for another. This not only improves retention across videos but also increases watch time per viewer because viewers naturally binge sequences. Topic sequencing turns your channel into a curriculum. It transforms each video into part of a larger transformation, increasing viewer loyalty and channel identity. The heart of sustainable long-form creation is **batching**. Batching means grouping tasks so you stay in the same creative state for longer periods instead of constantly switching. Script in batches. Film in batches. Edit in batches. Upload in batches. When you separate tasks, your mental load decreases. When you batch tasks, your efficiency skyrockets. Switching from scripting to filming to editing in the same day drains your cognitive energy, slows your progress, and increases stress. Batching allows you to create four to eight long-form videos in the same amount of time it once took you to create two. It is the single most powerful productivity multiplier for creators.

A crucial component of batching is **idea batching**. Set aside dedicated time to brainstorm ideas for the month. Don't filter yet. Don't edit yet. Just capture as many potential topics as possible. When you capture ideas in bursts, your creativity expands because your brain stays in ideation mode. Later, you filter the list through your content categories, select the strongest ideas, and sequence them into your content plan. Idea batching ensures you always have more content than you need, preventing panic and keeping your creativity abundant.

Another essential batching skill is **script batching**. Once your topics are selected, script several videos at once. Scripting multiple videos in a single sitting helps your voice remain consistent, your ideas sharpen, and your messaging become more cohesive. When you script one video at a time on different days, your tone and structure fluctuate. Script batching creates uniformity, rhythm, and clarity across your long-form content. It also reduces the mental friction of switching between writing and filming tasks.

From script batching comes the next step: **filming batching**. Once your scripts are ready, film multiple videos in one session. Set up your lights once. Set up your microphone once. Position your camera once. Check your framing once. Doing all of this for every single video individually wastes hours. But when you batch filming, you leverage your setup time efficiently and stay in performance flow. Filming back-to-back videos also improves on-camera presence because you warm up more naturally and maintain your energy across the session. This is what allows creators to publish weekly content while filming only one or two days per month.

After filming comes **editing batching**, which requires a similar mindset. Editing is mentally demanding, so batching reduces overwhelm. Instead of fully editing one video from start to finish before beginning the next, consider editing in layers: rough cuts for all videos, then b-roll placement for all videos, then transitions, then audio enhancements, then polishing. Layered batching prevents burnout by giving each editing stage a dedicated block of attention. It also dramatically increases your consistency in style, pacing, and visual language because you apply the same editing mindset across multiple videos.

Once your videos are edited, **upload batching** ensures your publishing schedule remains stable. Upload your videos early, schedule them in advance, write descriptions together, optimize metadata in a single session, and prepare thumbnails in cohesive batches so your channel maintains a consistent visual brand. Upload batching gives you the freedom to step away when needed without breaking consistency. Viewers trust creators who show up reliably. Batching is the key to staying reliable without sacrificing mental health.

The second major component of long-form sustainability is **repurposing**. Repurposing means taking one long-form video and transforming it into multiple pieces of content. You don't create more work—you extract more value from the work you already did. Long-form videos naturally produce dozens of moments worth sharing. Repurposing allows you to turn key insights, emotional moments, transitions, or story beats into short-form videos, reels, shorts, community posts, tweets, newsletters, or blog posts. Repurposing strengthens your reach by placing your best ideas across multiple platforms.

Repurposing works because long-form content contains depth. This depth lets you extract micro-stories, micro-insights, or micro-tutorials that stand alone effectively. When repurposing strategically, your long-form content becomes the root system of a multi-platform presence. Your videos become evergreen assets that continuously generate engagement. Repurposing also increases your discoverability—viewers may find your short-form content first and then move into your long-form videos for deeper connection.

One advanced strategy is creating **repurposing maps**, which outline exactly how each long-form video will produce multiple short-form clips. These maps include potential hook moments, emotional peaks, step-by-step segments, visual transitions, or especially insightful sentences. By identifying these moments at the scripting stage, you ensure your long-form videos are structured in a way that repurposing becomes effortless. This dramatically increases efficiency and multiplies your content output.

Finally, long-form content planning succeeds only when you build **a repeatable system**. Systems protect you from burnout. Systems make creativity sustainable. Systems create consistency even during chaotic moments in life. A system is a promise you make to your future self: you will not rely on willpower or inspiration—you will rely on a workflow that supports you. Long-form creators who build sustainable systems outlast everyone else. They grow steadily, strategically, effortlessly. When your long-form content becomes systematic, you unlock true creative freedom.

"The Month Everything Finally Became Easy"

For two years, Maya lived in a cycle of constant pressure. Every week felt like a race to come up with a new video idea, script it, film it, edit it, and upload it before the next deadline. Some weeks she made great content; other weeks she barely held things together. Her subscribers noticed the inconsistency. Her upload schedule slipped. Her stress rose. She loved creating videos, but the chaos was draining her passion. On the outside, her channel looked fine—but behind the scenes, she was exhausted.

The breaking point came during a month when three big projects collided at once. Maya found herself filming a video at 2 a.m. because she had fallen behind. She forgot lines, lost energy, stumbled through sentences, and eventually burst into tears in front of the camera. She shut the recording off and sat in silence. She realized this pace wasn't just unsustainable—it was killing her creativity. She didn't want to quit YouTube, but she couldn't keep living this way. Something had to change.

A few days later, she watched a behind-the-scenes video from a creator she admired. The creator explained how he planned and batched all his long-form content for the month in a single week. He scripted four videos in one day. Filmed them in two days. Edited them in layers across four days. And then uploaded everything at once. Maya stared at the screen in disbelief. He wasn't hustling every week—he was batching. Planning. Sequencing. Repurposing. It was the opposite of chaos. It was calm. It was efficient. It was sustainable.

Inspired, Maya grabbed a notebook and began building her first real content system. She wrote down content categories. She listed ideas without censoring herself. She circled the strongest ones and arranged them into a sequence. She scripted three videos in one sitting, amazed at how naturally her thoughts flowed when she wasn't under time pressure. The next day, she filmed all three videos with fresh energy and genuine enthusiasm. Her presence felt warm instead of rushed. Her words felt fluid instead of scattered. For the first time in years, filming felt enjoyable again.

Editing felt different too. Instead of trying to finish a video in one go, she edited in stages. First rough cuts. Then b-roll. Then audio tuning. Then transitions. Then polish. Each step had its own rhythm. Each step felt lighter. She wasn't racing—she was creating. By the end of the week, she had three completed videos scheduled. She looked at her YouTube queue with tears of relief. She had achieved something she once believed was impossible: she was ahead. The next month, Maya took it even further. She created a repurposing map for each long-form video, marking moments that could become shorts, reels, and posts. After uploading her long-form content, she turned each video into eight pieces of short-form content. Her reach exploded. Her channel grew faster. But more importantly, she felt calm for the first time in years. She had time to think. Time to rest. Time to create with intention instead of panic.

By the third month, Maya had become someone new. Her workflow was smooth, predictable, sustainable. She no longer feared the weekly upload deadline because her videos were always done far in advance. She filmed with joy. She edited with clarity. She wrote with flow. Each video felt better than the last—not because she worked harder, but because she worked smarter. Her viewers noticed the transformation. Comments poured in praising her consistency and renewed energy.

One evening, as she sat at her desk reviewing her upcoming videos, Maya realized she wasn't overwhelmed anymore. She wasn't drowning. She was thriving. For the first time, she understood what professional creators meant by "building a system." It wasn't about productivity hacks or rigid schedules.

It was about giving herself the structure she needed to create freely. It was about taking control of her time instead of letting panic control her.

She whispered to herself, almost in disbelief, “This is the month everything finally became easy.” And she knew she would never go back to the old way again.

Chapter 10

Monetization & Growth Systems: Turning Long-Form Videos into Income, Impact & Influence

Long-form video is the foundation of one of the most powerful income engines available to modern creators. Unlike short-form videos, which deliver bursts of attention, long-form content delivers depth, trust, emotional connection, and authority. These are the elements that drive monetization. When a viewer spends 10, 20, or 40 minutes with you, they bond with you in a way that no other content format can replicate. That bond is what opens the door to revenue streams such as ads, sponsorships, UGC deals, course sales, affiliate partnerships, coaching programs, digital products, and long-term brand building. Monetization is not the result of luck—it is the result of systems, frameworks, and long-term strategy applied consistently.

The first principle of long-form monetization is **value alignment**. The revenue you generate depends on how well your content aligns with the needs, desires, and problems of your audience. You do not need millions of subscribers to make substantial income—you need clear alignment. When your long-form videos consistently solve real problems, teach meaningful skills, or inspire transformation, your viewers naturally want more from you. Monetization becomes a natural extension rather than a forced offer. Value alignment is what turns views into subscribers, subscribers into fans, fans into customers, and customers into lifelong supporters of your work.

The second principle is **offer readiness**. Many creators fail to monetize because they produce content without having an ecosystem behind it. A monetization system requires an offer—something the viewer can purchase, join, or support. This could be a course, a membership, a product, a consulting service, a tool, a downloadable template, or a premium experience. The offer must be clear, relevant, and beneficial to the same viewer who enjoys your content. Long-form videos are the best environment to naturally introduce your offer through storytelling, teaching, soft mentions, or calls to action. The key is subtle integration rather than aggressive pitching.

Another essential principle is **audience segmentation**. Not every viewer wants the same thing. Some want deeper learning. Some want entertainment. Some want tools. Some want support. By creating different monetization paths tailored to different viewer segments, you maximize your revenue potential. For example, tutorials can lead to paid templates or courses. Story-based videos can lead to books or personal development programs. Gear reviews can lead to affiliate income. Business-focused content can lead to coaching or digital products. Segmentation ensures your monetization remains highly relevant to each type of viewer.

The heart of monetization is **trust**, and trust is built through consistency. When creators show up regularly, with high-quality long-form content that delivers value, viewers feel confident in them. Trust increases conversion rates across every revenue stream. A creator with fewer viewers but high trust can earn more than a creator with millions of passive viewers. Long-form videos deepen trust faster than any other content format because viewers spend extended time hearing your voice, absorbing your ideas, and learning from your expertise.

One of the most profitable long-form monetization strategies is **integrated storytelling**, where your offer or revenue stream is incorporated into the narrative of your video. Instead of forcing a pitch at the end, the offer becomes part of the value. You explain how you developed a skill, how your product was created, how your toolkit saves time, or how your course provides deeper guidance. The viewer sees the offer as part of the journey, not an interruption. This method increases conversions while maintaining viewer experience.

Another major monetization pathway is **affiliate revenue**. Affiliates allow you to earn income from recommending products, tools, software, or gear that your audience already wants. Long-form videos create the perfect environment for affiliate integration because viewers trust your judgment and appreciate detailed breakdowns. Reviews, tutorials, gear lists, buyer guides, and workflow videos all convert extremely well when paired with affiliate links. Transparency is key—share why you recommend the product, how you use it, and what the viewer should consider before purchasing.

Sponsorship deals represent another lucrative avenue, especially when aligned with your niche. Brands are willing to pay substantial amounts for long-form integration because your viewers are highly engaged. The value of your sponsorships increases dramatically when your retention rates are high and your niche is well-defined. The key to sponsorship success is selectivity—work only with brands that genuinely benefit your audience. This preserves trust and increases long-term opportunities.

A powerful monetization vehicle for creators is **YouTube Ads (AdSense)**. While ad revenue varies based on niche and watch time, long-form content typically earns higher CPMs because advertisers prefer videos where viewers are deeply engaged. The longer viewers watch, the more mid-roll ads

YouTube can serve, and the more money you earn. When your long-form structure, pacing, and production quality improve, so does your watch time—and thus your ad revenue. Ads may not be your primary monetization stream, but they become a stable, passive foundation.

Beyond ads and sponsorships, **digital products** are one of the most scalable and profitable revenue streams. Templates, scripts, guides, presets, editing tools, b-roll packs, or planning worksheets can be created once and sold indefinitely. Long-form videos provide the perfect place to demonstrate or reference these products naturally. When a viewer sees how your tool or asset improves their workflow, they are far more likely to purchase it. Digital products scale infinitely without requiring additional time per customer.

Another high-impact strategy is **courses and educational programs**. Long-form video provides the ideal foundation for selling courses because viewers already trust your teaching ability. If your long-form videos deliver insight, your paid course delivers transformation. Courses help viewers achieve deeper results than they can get for free, and viewers appreciate the structure, clarity, and step-by-step guidance. When marketed properly, courses often become a creator's top revenue driver.

For creators who want to build deeper connections, **memberships and communities** provide recurring revenue. Memberships may include exclusive videos, livestreams, Q&A sessions, behind-the-scenes content, templates, or personal support. Long-form content attracts viewers who want more from you, making memberships a natural extension. Communities also reinforce binge-watching behavior because viewers feel part of something meaningful.

A critical component of monetization is **conversion moments**, which are small opportunities throughout your video to direct the viewer toward your offer. These are not sales pitches—they are invitations. They may include mentioning a tool you built, referencing a course, highlighting a recommended product, or inviting viewers to explore more resources. Conversion moments must feel natural, helpful, and optional. When placed strategically, they generate revenue without harming retention.

Finally, long-form monetization thrives through **systems**, not random attempts. Systems ensure that every video has a purpose, every purpose connects to an offer, and every offer fits into a long-term brand strategy. Systems turn your channel into a business. Systems create compounding results. Systems turn creativity into predictable income. When you design monetization intentionally, your channel becomes a powerful engine that grows your impact and income for years. Long-form creators who build monetization systems become unstoppable. Their content attracts loyal viewers. Their viewers support their work. Their offers provide transformation. Their brand grows. Their income stabilizes. Monetization isn't a final step—it's the natural outcome of thoughtful, value-driven long-form creation. And once you master it, you are no longer just a creator. You are a leader of a thriving creative business.

"The Video That Paid the Rent"

When Jonathan first started his YouTube channel, he dreamed about the day it would earn enough money to support him. But for years, the dream felt distant. His videos gained views, but the money trickled in slowly—too slowly. He wondered what he was doing wrong. He uploaded consistently. He improved his filming techniques. He upgraded his gear. But his income remained unpredictable. Some months brought small spikes, others dropped to almost nothing. Jonathan began to wonder if maybe he just wasn't meant to make a living through YouTube.

Everything changed one night when he watched a video from a creator he admired. The creator explained how long-form content wasn't just about views—it was about trust. And trust was the foundation of every revenue stream. "People buy from people they trust," the creator said. "And trust is earned by spending time with them." Jonathan paused the video and stared at the screen. That sentence felt like lightning in his chest. He realized he had been chasing views instead of relationships. His content had value, but he wasn't aligning it with offers or solving specific problems. He had been creating videos without a system.

That realization sparked a transformation. Jonathan spent the next week planning his first real monetization strategy. He reviewed all his past videos and identified what his viewers cared about most. He noticed patterns—specific topics that sparked conversation, questions, and deeper interest. He used those patterns to create his first digital product: a simple toolkit that solved a common problem his viewers faced. He priced it modestly, not expecting much. Then he made a long-form video where he shared the journey that led him to create the tool—not as a pitch, but as part of the story.

When he uploaded the video, he felt nervous. He didn't want viewers to think he was selling out. But something unexpected happened. Comments began rolling in: "This is exactly what I needed," "Thank you for making this," "I'm purchasing right now," "This makes so much sense." The next morning, Jonathan woke up to more notifications than he had ever seen. His email inbox was full of purchase confirmations. His heart pounded as he checked his dashboard. For the first time in his journey, his video had made more money than he had earned in the previous two months combined. That was the moment he understood the power of trust. His viewers weren't paying for a product—they were paying because they believed in him. They felt connected. They valued his guidance. The video wasn't just content; it was a bridge between him and the people he served. With renewed motivation, he continued building his monetization ecosystem. He created an affiliate hub with products he genuinely loved and used. He partnered with a brand whose mission aligned with his audience's needs. He developed a beginner-friendly course that expanded on what his videos taught.

As his system grew, something incredible happened. His income became stable. Predictable. Instead of hoping a video would go viral, he followed a strategy that generated revenue from multiple sources. His long-form videos became the engine that powered everything. Each new upload strengthened viewer trust. Each story he shared created deeper resonance. Each tutorial led to tools, resources, or programs that improved his viewers' lives. Jonathan no longer felt like he was guessing—he was growing with intention.

One afternoon, he sat at his kitchen table reviewing his earnings dashboard. He noticed a simple line item that made him smile: the digital product he launched months ago had paid enough that week to cover his rent entirely. He closed his eyes and let the realization settle. It wasn't about the money—it was about what the money represented. Freedom. Stability. Validation. He whispered quietly, "This is real now." The dream that once felt distant was becoming his life.

As his channel continued to grow, Jonathan built a community that trusted him deeply. He focused on teaching, supporting, and inspiring rather than selling. And because he put his viewers' needs first, his business flourished. The memory of the video that paid his rent stayed with him. It wasn't the most polished video he ever made. It wasn't the most viral. But it was the first time he understood what long-form content was truly capable of. It wasn't just entertainment—it was transformation.

And from that day forward, Jonathan approached every video with a new mindset: not "How do I get views?" but "How do I help people so deeply that trust becomes inevitable?" The answer changed everything.

Epilogue

The Creator You Become in the Process

When you first begin the journey into long-form video creation, it is easy to believe that the goal is the video itself—the perfect script, the perfect shot, the perfect edit, the perfect upload. But as you complete this book, you now understand something deeper: long-form video is not just about the content you create. It is about the creator you become along the way. It is about patience, discipline, confidence, communication, creativity, trust-building, and the quiet art of showing up consistently. Long-form content does not just shape your channel; it reshapes your identity. It challenges your comfort zones, strengthens your resilience, and deepens your sense of purpose. Every step—from scripting to filming to editing to speaking to structuring—forces you to develop skills that extend far beyond YouTube.

Long-form creators grow in ways that most people never see. The audience sees the polished final product, but behind every video lies a version of you learning, stumbling, refining, and rising. They see the clarity of your message, but they don't see the hours you spent rewriting the script until the ideas felt honest. They see your confident presence, but they don't see the early days when the camera made your voice shake. They see smooth pacing and clean edits, but they don't see the nights you stared at your timeline, wondering if you were cut out for this. They see your growth, but they can never fully understand the depth of work that shaped it. That unseen work is the true story of long-form creation—the slow transformation that turns you into a communicator, a storyteller, and a leader.

As you master long-form video production, something remarkable begins to happen: your content becomes a mirror of your evolution. Each video reflects a new level of clarity in your voice, a new layer of intention in your structure, and a new expression of confidence in your delivery. Over time, you notice that filming feels natural, editing feels intuitive, and speaking feels fluid. What once felt intimidating now feels like home. Long-form creation quietly rewires your mind. Your thoughts become more organized, your storytelling improves organically, and your ability to explain complex ideas strengthens without you even noticing. This internal refinement is the true reward of consistent creation—your mind becomes sharper, your voice becomes stronger, your message becomes clearer.

But long-form content shapes more than just your skillset. It shapes your relationship with your audience. Viewers who watch your long-form videos are not casual scrollers—they are companions on your journey. They spend time with you, learn from you, and trust you. They hear your voice during their mornings, their workouts, their commutes, and their quiet nights. Long-form viewers form a bond that feels almost personal, and that bond becomes the foundation of your brand, your community, and your long-term impact. This connection is not built through algorithms or viral moments—it is built through consistency, honesty, presence, and genuine care for the people you serve. Long-form content is the closest digital equivalent to sitting across from someone and having a real conversation. That is why it is so powerful.

As you continue creating long-form videos, you will also experience the quiet power of compound growth. At first, your videos may feel invisible. You may wonder if anyone is watching. You may question if your work matters. But long-form content compounds silently. Videos you created months ago continue gaining views. Tutorials become evergreen assets. Stories continue resonating. Lessons continue serving new viewers. Long-form videos age like books—they become part of your legacy. They work for you long after you upload them. And as this library of value grows, your channel evolves from a project into a digital ecosystem that supports your creativity and your livelihood. Each video becomes a long-term seed that continues to bear fruit.

Over time, something even deeper happens: long-form video becomes a pathway to who you were meant to be. It gives you a channel to express your voice, your ideas, your insights, your perspective. It becomes a place where your knowledge becomes impact, where your story becomes inspiration, where your challenges become lessons for others. In a world filled with noise, long-form content allows you to create meaning—intentional, organized, lasting meaning. It becomes your way of contributing to the world. And in return, the world pays you back through trust, loyalty, and opportunities you never imagined possible.

There will be days when you feel tired, when creativity feels heavy, when life gets in the way. But the creator you have become through this journey will know how to rise. You will rely on systems instead of stress. You will rely on structure instead of panic. You will rely on presence instead of perfection. Long-form creation develops not just skill, but resilience. Not just strategy, but identity. And once you understand that, you realize that this path is not just about mastering video—it is about mastering your ability to communicate, influence, and elevate others.

As this book comes to a close, remember that the next chapter of your creative journey begins now. You have the tools, the structure, the psychology, the strategy, and the skillset to create long-form videos that change lives, build businesses, and leave a legacy. You are no longer guessing; you are designing. You are no longer experimenting blindly; you are executing with purpose. You are no longer hoping for growth; you are building a system that guarantees it. Long-form creation is no longer something you are trying to figure out—it is something you are becoming exceptional at.

The future of your channel is not determined by the algorithm—it is determined by your willingness to show up with clarity, intention, and consistency. You now possess the mindset of a creator who understands the real game: long-form content is not about chasing attention; it is about cultivating influence. It is not about virality; it is about impact. It is not about perfection; it is about presence. And from this point forward, every video you create carries the potential to reach someone at the right moment, shift their perspective, or give them the guidance they've been searching for.

You are stepping into a new identity now. You are becoming the creator who doesn't wait for inspiration—you build systems that allow inspiration to thrive. You are becoming the creator who doesn't hide behind uncertainty—you lead with clarity and confidence. You are becoming the creator who doesn't rely on luck—you rely on skill, intention, and purpose. Long-form video is your stage, your canvas, your opportunity, and your legacy. And with every upload, you are writing the story of your growth—not just as a creator, but as a communicator, a teacher, and a leader.

The journey does not end here. It begins here. Your next video, your next story, your next transformation is waiting. The world is waiting. And now, you are ready to step forward and create not just content—but impact. Not just videos—but experiences. Not just views—but lives changed. Your long-form legacy starts now.

www.ingramcontent.com/pod-product-compliance
Lightning Source LLC
LaVergne TN
LVHW022008200926
848481LV00007B/2278
* 9 7 9 8 2 9 5 4 7 2 1 1 4 *